Rain Forest Rescue

Anna Mackenzie
illustrated by Helen Humphries

Learning Media®

Contents

1. Far from Home 3
2. Halfway House 11
3. Bat Island 17
4. Back to the Compound 24
   Find Out More 29

1. Far from Home

Sara folded the letter. Her friend Amy had written about going sledding with her older brothers. Sara couldn't imagine snow. Even with the fan whirring rapidly, she felt sticky and uncomfortable.

When her mom had told her that they were moving to Kalimantan for two years, Sara hadn't known what to think. She'd looked up Kalimantan on the Internet and found that it was in Indonesia on the island of Borneo, but that hadn't helped much. It had seemed so strange and far away. The only thing she was sure of was that home was thousands of miles away across the Pacific Ocean.

Her mom had given her books to read and had told her about the Orangutan Rehabilitation Center. She'd explained that the center cared for orangutans that had been rescued from captivity. Their goal was to release the orangutans back into the jungle, but first, they had to prepare them for life in the wild. Sara's mom would be working as a vet in the clinic, caring for any sick or injured orangutans that were brought in.

Sara stared out of the window of the hut that she shared with her mom near the orangutan nursery. Outside, the heat waited like a living thing, ready to pounce. Beyond the scattering of low buildings that filled the compound, the jungle rose up in a hundred different colors of green. Although she would never admit it to her mom, Sara secretly liked the jungle. She liked its unexpected colors and its rich texture of smells, as well as the huge scale of things: giant flowers, fat vines, leaves so broad you could use them as umbrellas.

Sara sighed and turned away from the window. One thing she didn't much like was orangutans. As far as she was concerned, there was something freaky about the big apes. They were almost like humans, but their arms were too long, and their eyes were so sad that they made Sara feel uncomfortable. "Orangutans are our closest relatives," her mom had told her. Sara had wrinkled her nose and thought about her cousins back home. She knew it was awful what people did to the orangutans – killing mothers and stealing their babies for pets and destroying so much forest that there were no longer safe places for the wild orangutans to live – but they sure didn't feel like relatives to her.

Sara's mom put her head around the door of the hut. "Come and look!" she cried, smiling with delight. "Bo's learning to climb!"

Reluctantly, Sara followed her mother to the play enclosure. The baby orangutan had swung himself up the rope mesh and looked as if he had no idea how he'd done it. His long fingers were wrapped around the rope, and one of his legs was stretched sideways as if he were trying to step out onto the air.

7

An older orangutan, Mimi, climbed down the branch that leaned against the platform, watched Bo for a minute, and then swung one of her long arms toward him. Sara thought she was going to push him off. "She's encouraging him to come onto the platform," said Sara's mom. "He only needs to climb another few rungs." Her mom sounded excited. "This is as high as he's ever gone."

Sara frowned. Bo was only 4 feet off the ground.

Suddenly, he seemed to notice Mimi, and he stretched his arms toward her. As he did so, he let go of the rope and tumbled in a hairy red ball back to the ground. Karim, who worked in the nursery, went over to check that Bo was all right.

"Try climbing up the net," Sara's mom suggested to Karim. "He might climb with you."

There were thirteen orangutans in the nursery, all rescued from captivity. They had been taken from their mothers at a young age, so none of them had learned the most basic things that orangutans need to know. They couldn't search for food or build their own sleeping nests, and some, like Bo, couldn't even climb.

Privately, Sara thought that Bo – now curled into a ball – was a hopeless case. When he first arrived at the center, he had been very sick: his hair was falling out, and his skin had red flaking patches. Often, the orangutans were poorly treated by the poachers who stole them from the forest or by the people who bought them as pets. Like the others, Bo had been nursed back to health during his time in quarantine, but he was no longer making progress.

Sara shrugged. "I'm going to finish my letter to Amy," she said. Her mom glanced around, her forehead creased in concern, but just at that moment, two more young orangutans appeared, and her attention immediately switched back to the apes. Sara sighed and turned away.

2. Halfway House

As Sara walked across the compound, a young woman came out of the central office building. It was Casriani, one of the park rangers.

"Hello, Sara," she called. "I'm going to the halfway house today to check on Kong and Kapi, and then I'm taking the boat to the observation deck on Bat Island. Would you like to come?"

Sara shrugged. "OK," she replied. Anything was better than hanging around the compound.

Kong and Kapi had been released from the nursery two weeks ago. They were now at the halfway house, where they could roam around the forest during the day but still come back to the house to sleep at night.

A raised boardwalk led Sara and Casriani from the central compound to the halfway house, where a ranger was checking on Kong.

While the two adults chatted, Sara sat on the edge of the viewing platform and stared into the rich foliage around her. The air was alive with birdcalls and the creaking and shrilling of insects. The forest, too, seemed to talk. A breeze swayed through the upper story of the trees, and the rustling and sighing of the leaves drifted gently down through the lower levels of the rain forest.

Bright butterflies and the brilliant flash of a hornbill's showy wings caught her eye. There was so much to look at. It was hard to believe that people were destroying it. The rain forest was being logged and burned at an incredible rate, and thousands of species of plants and animals, not just the orangutans, were in danger.

Suddenly, Sara noticed a swooping red figure in the trees above. The orangutan looked right at home, swinging gracefully between the looping vines. Casriani had seen him too. "There's Kapi," she said with a smile. "We'd better go. We don't want to encourage him to come to us now that he's learning to take care of himself," she explained as they climbed down the steps from the halfway house.

Despite herself, Sara was interested. "You still feed them though, don't you?" she asked.

Casriani nodded, leading the way down to a track along the forest floor. "Less and less as they get used to finding their own food. By the time we move them to the halfway house, they've learned most of the skills they need. It's just a matter of confidence."

Sara suddenly felt a little sorry for the creatures. "If they've been with humans for most of their lives, isn't it hard for them to suddenly have to survive all on their own?" she asked.

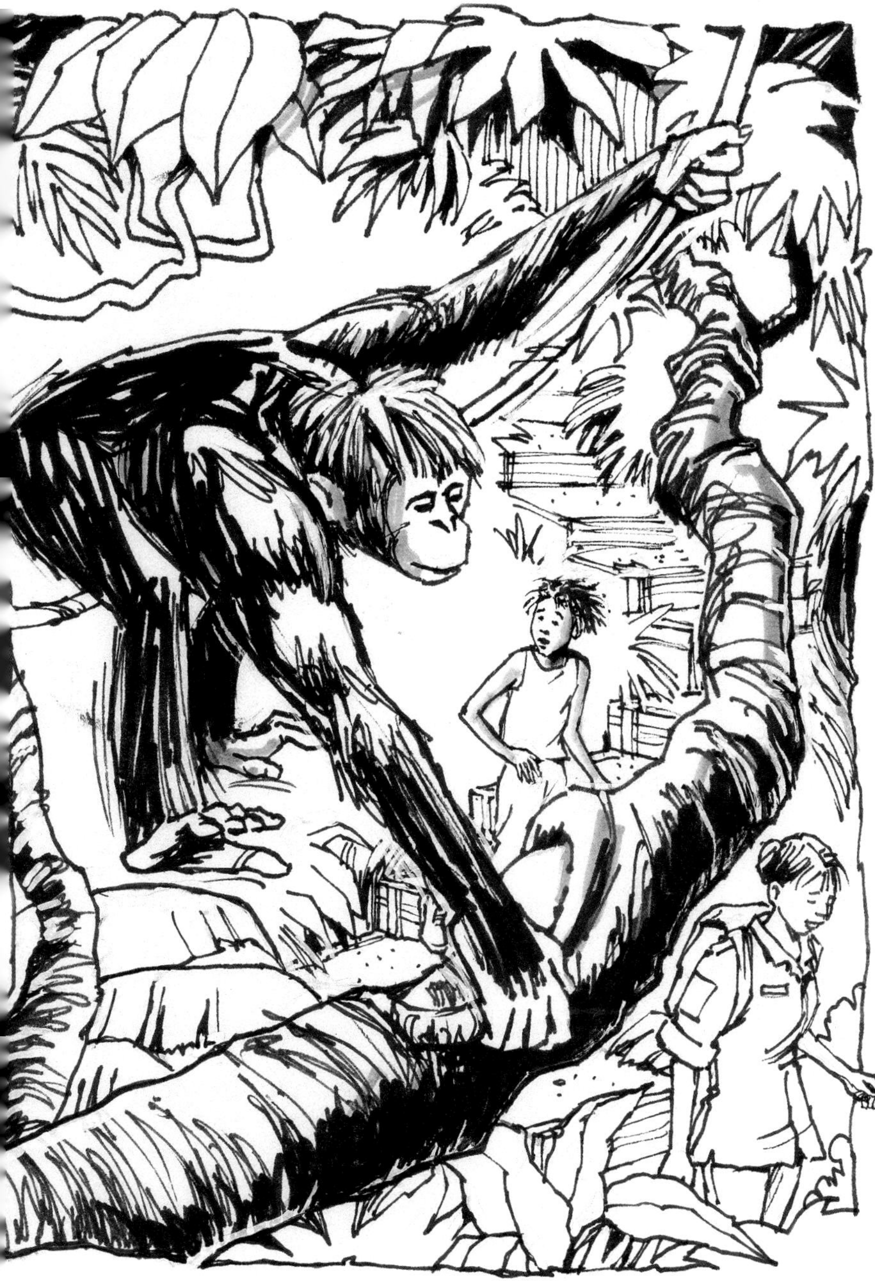

Casriani paused. "Hard, yes. That's why we go slowly and watch to make sure they're adjusting well." Sara nodded. Above their heads, Kapi was holding a thin trunk with one arm and both feet, leaning out sideways so that he swayed to and fro, watching them.

"Some can't adjust to the wild at all," Casriani added. "They aren't able to give up people."

"Is that why there's still an older female in the nursery?" Sara asked. "Doesn't she want to leave?"

"Mimi? She likes to help with the babies," Casriani answered. "Your mom thinks we'll get her back into the wild one day, but for now, she's learning parenting skills. When we release her, she'll be able to find a mate and have a baby of her own."

They walked silently along the track to the river, sweat trickling down their backs. Sara usually felt calm in the cool shelter of the trees, but not today. Thoughts of orangutans kept swinging through her head.

3. Bat Island

It was a short journey by boat down the river to Bat Island, where older orangutans were released into the forest, and then a twenty-minute walk to the observation deck. As they reached the deck, Pasal, the island ranger, called a greeting to Sara and Casriani. They climbed the ladder to what seemed like an oversized tree house. Sara felt a little dizzy as she looked down.

"We need to be quiet," Casriani warned. "We're here to watch."

Sara nodded and settled herself. The heat felt like a blanket wrapped around her, and the gentle sounds of the rain forest soothed her. She felt sleepy, and before she knew it, her eyes were closed.

A sharp noise woke her. Sara sat up in surprise. Casriani was scanning the trees around them and let out a sudden cry. Following her pointing finger, Sara easily picked out the orangey-red of an orangutan's shaggy coat, little more than a hundred yards from the platform. "She fell," Casriani said tersely. "There's something wrong."

The orangutan was half lying across a branch, one arm dangling while the other stretched above to a hanging vine. As they watched, the fingers uncurled, and the orangutan slipped from the branch. She fell through the trees in a series of crashes, her body battering against branches and trunks. With a hollow thump, they heard her hit the ground far below. The forest erupted in a series of wild distress calls. Sara's heart was beating hard.

"Quick!" Casriani cried. Sara hurried down the ladder after Casriani and Pasal. She felt weak and shaky. When they reached the orangutan and she saw the battered body up close, her insides seemed to squeeze into a tight, painful ball.

Casriani knelt by the figure that lay twisted on the ground. Pasal's fingers were pressed gently against the orangutan's neck. After a moment, he grunted and spoke briefly in Bahasa Malay. Casriani nodded, her eyes clouded.

"What?" Sara asked, barely able to force the question from her tight throat. Pasal was running his hands expertly along the orangutan's limbs.

"She's not dead," said Casriani, "but she has many broken bones."

"Bones can be fixed," said Sara.

Casriani nodded. "There's an older injury," she said. "Pasal thinks it's a gunshot wound." Sara looked to where Casriani was pointing. The orangutan's left leg was scabbed and swollen. "She has an infection – it's probably why she fell," Casriani added, gently stroking the orangutan's head. The creature's eyes remained closed.

"Why? Who would do that?" Sara asked.

"Poachers," Casriani replied.

As they worked to make a stretcher, Sara couldn't help feeling that she was being watched. Each time she looked around, there was no one, but the feeling wouldn't go away.

The orangutan moaned as Pasal lifted her onto the makeshift stretcher. Sara felt useless, trailing behind Pasal and Casriani as they carried the orangutan back along the trail to the observation deck. She still couldn't shake the feeling that they weren't alone. Once, there was a sound like a branch snapping, and she spun around, but there was no one there.

21

When they reached the observation deck, Pasal and Casriani lowered the stretcher to the ground and climbed up the ladder to the deck to radio ahead. Sitting beside the injured orangutan, Sara felt tears welling up in her eyes. The animal's breathing was hoarse and shallow, and one of her long arms was awkwardly bent. Sara squatted on the ground, folding her arms around her legs and tucking her head onto her knees in a pose similar to the one Bo had used after he fell from the net earlier that morning.

Suddenly, Sara felt the watching eyes more strongly than ever. Her heart began to pound. Casriani and Pasal were inside the shelter, but there was someone nearby, she just knew it – someone who had followed them as they carried the stretcher along the trail. Sara took a deep breath and, trying to appear casual, stared into the lush foliage around her.

Suddenly, she saw it: a flash of movement and color. She was about to cry out when she realized what she was seeing among the leaves. With a gasp, Sara froze.

4. Back to the Compound

Sara stayed completely still as a baby orangutan crept cautiously toward the stretcher and huddled against the older creature's body. "No sudden movements, Sara," called Casriani quietly as she climbed slowly down the ladder. "She's just a baby. This must be her mother."

Sara let her fingers touch the mother's shaggy side. She could feel the creature's chest rising in short panting breaths and the heat of the infection that was raging in her body. The baby orangutan beside her didn't react as Sara reached out to stroke its arm. It seemed to be in shock.

It had been the young orangutan's eyes that Sara had felt as it followed them through the rain forest. She wondered how she would have felt if this had been her mother, carried off by strangers.

The youngster flinched, leaning forward across its mother's body, as Sara lifted her hand to stroke its head.

As gently as she could, Sara took it into her arms. Her heart was beating hard – so was the baby orangutan's. The youngster huddled against her, lifting two thin arms and wrapping them tightly around her neck.

"We must go," Casriani said. "The sooner we get the mother to the clinic, the more chance she has." Sara nodded, following close beside the stretcher as they walked swiftly back to the boat. The baby orangutan held tight to her neck, its eyes never leaving its mother. Sara was tired and hot, but she walked fast. At least one life, if not two, depended on her.

Later that day, Sara visited the clinic to check on the new arrivals. Her mom greeted her with a smile. "You'll be pleased to hear that your little friend is fine," she said.

"What about her mother?" Sara asked.

"We're doing everything we can," she replied. "She's badly injured, but at least we have the infection under control. They were both lucky that you found them when you did," she added.

Sara frowned. "Why do people want them as pets?" she asked. "Don't they know it's illegal? Don't they understand that orangutans are an endangered species?"

"Why, I do believe I have a convert on my hands," Sara's mom said wryly. Sara could feel a hot flush creeping up her neck. "I thought you didn't like orangutans," her mom continued, eyebrow raised.

Just then, Casriani handed the baby orangutan to Sara, saving her from answering. The young orangutan wrapped an arm around her neck before turning to study Sara's mother.

"She likes you," her mom said.

"They're cute when they're small," Sara replied. "I guess that's why people want them as pets. They don't stay small, though."

"No, they don't," her mom agreed, "and they have a right to freedom."

Sara stroked the orangutan's head, thinking how close this beautiful creature had come to losing not just her freedom but also her life.

Watching them, her mom became thoughtful. "You know, it's possible that young orangutans respond differently to children than to adults," she said. "If you wanted," she added hesitantly, "you could help out in the nursery sometimes."

Sara nodded, returning her mother's smile as the young orangutan rested her soft head on Sara's shoulder. "I think I'd like that," she agreed.

WHAT'S THE BACKGROUND?

Orangutans

In the Malay language, "orangutan" means "man of the forest." Orangutans are the largest animals that climb trees. They swing from branch to branch using their strong arms, which can grow up to 6 feet (1.8 meters) long. They make nests in the trees to sleep in, and they hardly ever climb down to the ground.

The number of orangutans left in the wild is falling fast, and they are now in danger of becoming extinct. The main reason for this is the destruction of their home — the rain forest. In 1997 and 1998, there were large fires in Borneo that forced many orangutans out of the forests. Humans are making the problem worse by cutting down trees for timber. Another problem the orangutans face is poaching — many are taken and killed for food or sold as pets.

Rehabilitation centers, like the one in this story, prepare orangutans that have been kept as pets to live back in the wild. They help to rescue the orangutans and then teach them how to take care of themselves.

Find Out More

LOOKING CLOSER

Kalimantan

Orangutans once lived all over Southeast Asia, but today, they are found only on the islands of Sumatra and Borneo. Sara's mom works in an orangutan rehabilitation center in Kalimantan, the central and southern part of the island of Borneo.

The rain forests on Borneo are home to many different kinds of animals. Not only orangutans, but also rhinoceroses, giant moths, flying squirrels, and two thousand different kinds of trees can be found there. There may be thousands of different plants and animals on Borneo that haven't been discovered.

Find Out More

Find Out More

MAKING CONNECTIONS

Tigers in Danger

It's not only orangutans that are in danger of becoming extinct: many kinds of animals around the world are falling in number as their habitats are destroyed.

Tigers are now very rare in the wild. They are found only in Asia, and scientists think that there are fewer than 7,500 left. In the last seventy years, three kinds of tiger have already become extinct.

Tigers and orangutans face the same kinds of problems. The forests they live in are getting smaller and smaller, and people hunt them, even though it's against the law. A tiger's eyes, whiskers, bones, and claws are used in some traditional medicines, so hunters can ask high prices for them.